Laxey

HOME OF THE WORLD'S LARGEST WORKING WATERWHEEL

ANDREW SCARFFE

Published by:

Lily Publications, PO Box 33, Ramsey, Isle of Man IM99 4LP

Tel: +44 (0) 1624 898446   Fax: +44 (0) 1624 898449

E-mail: info@lilypublications.co.uk   Website: www.lilypublications.co.uk

INTRODUCTION

I can still recall my excitement when, as a young boy, my grandmother gave me an old postcard of a Manx Electric Railway tram at Dhoon Glen. It was post-marked 17th July, 1908 and as I was only nine years old at the time, the postcard fascinated me as it seemingly belonged to an unimaginably distant time in the past. The reason I can so clearly remember the year that I was given the postcard was because I wrote my name, address and the date on its rear with a felt pen…

The acquisition of this postcard sparked an interest in collecting old pictures of Laxey, in particular the Laxey Wheel and the Manx Electric Railway in which I have been interested, or perhaps more accurately obsessed by, for as long as I can remember. Nearly forty years later I still gain the same excitement from acquiring another previously unknown picture of Laxey or the railways.

I was delighted when Miles Cowsill asked me to produce a picture book of old Laxey. It was an excuse to again wade through my photograph collection and to also visit friends and look through their postcard collections and photograph albums. All generously gave me copies of their pictures. My very grateful thanks therefore are due to Ann Haddock, Michael Leece, Peter Kelly, Mike Kelly, Edwin Kinrade, Les and Sue Hutchin, John

As 'New Laxey' quickly expanded, the main centre of population was now somewhat distant from Lonan Parish Church. At the instigation of the Laxey Mining Company, a new village church was constructed and consecrated as Christ Church in 1856. It was built on the lawns of the Mine Captain's house with a driveway leading in from the New Road. In 1898 the gardens and lawns were chosen as the location of a new station for both the coastal and mountain tramways. Such was the march of progress that the sole voice of objection to the new station was that of the vicar. The Mine Captain's house survives today as the Mines Tavern.
(Photo: Authors Collection)

Kinrade, Ray Stanfield, Les Clarke, Brian McMullen, Irene Simpson, Ted Gray, Linda Clague, Norman McKibbin, Mike Scarffe, Ken Kinrade, Edith and Colvyn Quaggin, John Corlett, Richard Davis, Ian and Sally McMullen, Bill Barlow, Margaret Sadler, John Kneale and Maureen Thornley. Sadly John Kinrade and Brian McMullen passed away during the production time of this book.

I still remain very keen to add to my collection and would ask that anyone who has suitable pictures to please contact me via email thescarffes@manx.net.

It has been an extremely difficult task to choose which illustrations to include in the book; there were many worthy examples which a lack of space dictated had to fall by the wayside. Where possible I have attempted to use illustrations which have not previously appeared in print. The quality of some may be poorer than may be desired but their historical significance merits inclusion. Sadly, the space available has also dictated that the content has had to be limited to coverage of Laxey Village and only a couple of pictures are included of topics within Lonan Parish, of which the village is a part.

Finally, I would like to dedicate this book to Nichola, Francesca and Bethany.

– Andrew Scarffe, 2014

Laxey

It was over a thousand years ago that the invading Vikings named this ancient settlement 'Lax-voe', meaning 'Salmon River', in acknowledgement of the abundance of the salmon found in the river flowing down the valley from the Island's only mountain. Its name, Snaefell, is also of Norse origin meaning 'Snow Mountain'. Situated at the river mouth next to the large bay, early man found the place ideal for their basic needs of food, shelter and safety. The bay abounded with fish and the hillsides, though steep in places, provided fertile ground for growing crops and grazing animals.

Laxa or Laxey, as it was to become known, changed very little over the following millennium. A traveller to the village in 1797 recorded that Laxey was a village of only 30 cottages with a flax mill, a tucking mill, three corn mills and a bridge of four arches crossing the river. A single packhorse road, narrow, steep and frequently dangerous, connected with Douglas to the South and Ramsey to the north. Small boats plied up and down the coast.

This was to change with the discovery, at around the same time, of deposits of rich lead ore and its subsequent mining was to change the village significantly over the next few decades. Waterwheels, shafts and winding houses appeared on the hillsides, the washing floors were constructed on the lower slopes of the valley and a huge pile of waste stone from the mine eventually towered over nearby houses.

A new road, a name by which it is still known, was built in 1854 on a much easier gradient around the valley sides to replace the old packhorse road. New Road gave access to additional land for development and new houses, shops, pubs, a church and a school were built to serve the rapidly increasing population. In effect there were now two villages, Old Laxey by the harbour and New Laxey near the mine. By the mid 1870s, when the Great Laxey Mine was one of the richest and certainly the most famous metal mine in the United Kingdom, a 1000 men (and a few women) were employed in mining in the Laxey area.

From the early 1880s, the mine's fortunes began to slowly dwindle which was to finally result in closure in April 1930. Fortunately, as the mining industry declined, the Isle of Man was emerging as an immensely popular tourist destination. In July 1894, the electric tramway from Douglas to Laxey was opened and many, many thousands of visitors came to the village. The Laxey Glen Gardens had been opened in the 1870s and was now one of the Island's most popular tourist destinations. Hotels and boarding houses were built. Lady Isabella, the Laxey Wheel, had attracted visitors to Laxey ever since it had been built in 1854 to pump flood water out of the lead mine. Fortunately the waterwheel, the biggest in the world, was privately preserved as the village's foremost tourist attraction.

Following the end of the Second World War the Island's tourism enjoyed a brief period of immense popularity as many hundreds of thousands of visitors seeking an escape from the post war austerity returned to the Island. But the boom years of Manx Tourism passed and a gradual decline in the number of visitors began and which was to last some fifty years. Amidst severe financial difficulty, the Manx Electric Railway had been nationalised in 1957.

Despite the decline in overall visitor numbers, Laxey remains a very popular destination for visitors; where else can one travel on the world's oldest operating electric trams to the world's largest waterwheel? Although the population has slowly increased since the 1970s, Laxey retains its unrivalled scenic beauty and village community spirit. One thousand years after the Vikings first landed, it continues to be an idyllic place to live.

3

From ancient times, a 'gathering' or fair, where livestock and produce was bought, sold and exchanged, was held annually during the first week of August next to the river and beach. Having its origins in a religious ceremony celebrating the Patron Saint of the Parish, the gathering was also an opportunity for relaxation and enjoyment. In this drawing of the fair, dating to about 1835, rows of stalls line the river bank, a tradition recalled today by the name of Tent Road which runs along the harbour side. A traditional fair was last held in the early 1900s. (Photo: Authors Collection.)

From both sides of the valley, the pack horse road descended steeply to the Laxey River which was crossed by a ford until the present stone bridge was built; it was mentioned for the first time in 1732 but its date of construction may have been much earlier. For centuries an inn or public house has stood on the river bank next to this crossing point. Descent of the packhorse road by horse drawn coach, in the winter months especially, must have been a somewhat thrilling experience to say the least! Clay Head to the south of the bay afforded some protection to the beach but inshore easterly gales frequently battered the small village. (Photo: Authors Collection)

Although little more than a small wooden jetty, the rudimentary facilities were formally designated as a harbour in 1766. In 1792 it was noted that twenty large fishing boats sailed from the harbour and that a herring curing house was situated close by. Despite the ever increasing quantities of ore being shipped from the Laxey Mine, the first proper harbour facilities were not provided until 1861. In the absence of government funding the cost was met by public subscription instigated by Mine Captain Richard Rowe. In this picture fishing vessels can be seen moored against the breakwater. (Photo: Authors Collection)

As a result of Captains Rowe's efforts, a stone pier was constructed to protect a new small harbour to its rear which became known as 'Rowe's Dock'. Although this was a much needed improvement, the harbour remained at the mercy of inshore gales and numerous vessels were damaged. The complete destruction of the steamer Viking, fully loaded with 280 tons of lead ore, at the harbour mouth in March 1889 finally prompted the construction in 1892 of the breakwater linking with the 'Cairn' or headland. The absence of vegetation in the fields and the minimal tree growth is particularly apparent in this aerial view dating to about 1936.
(Photo: Authors Collection)

7

Viewed from the Cairn in 1904, the harbour side was dominated by the large warehouse built by Captain Rowe in 1865 to store grain for the Laxey Glen Mill. The stone-walled compound to the front of the warehouse was known as the 'Jack Yard' and was used to store zinc ore, known as 'jack', prior to shipping to smelting works in South Wales. The smaller warehouse building on the sea front was used to store coal; it is now a public shelter and café. (Photo: Collection, Brian McMullen)

From the same location, the photographer has now turned his camera to look in a westerly direction towards the Laxey Valley. At 'Rowe's Dock' work is underway to widen Tent Road and build a new supporting wall. Later the harbour would be properly enclosed to the rear and a stone wall built in the river bed to prevent flood water scouring the foundations of the pier. It was somewhat ironic that the improvement works to the harbour were finally concluded just as the Laxey Mine closed. (Photo: Collection, Brian McMullen)

Following closure of the Great Laxey Mine the harbour initially remained fairly busy, particularly with the importation of coal for the local coal merchants and the Manx Electric Railway and grain for the Laxey Glen Mill. However, usage declined and it was finally closed to commercial trade on 1st April, 1973. The Ramsey Steamship Company's 346 ton Ben Veg, which had been built specifically for accessing small coastal harbours, had the honour of carrying the very last cargo into the harbour, a shipment of grain for the mill. The harbour remains in use as a popular berth for small pleasure craft. (Photo: W S Basnett)

Viewed from the northern side of the river looking towards the sea, the harbour area is dominated by the sailing ship Daisy which lay abandoned there from 1908 until August 1912 when she was towed to Ramsey and scrapped. (Photo: Authors Collection)

Prior to the construction of the promenade, the beach (and often the sea!) reached to the front doors of the cottages built on the seafront. Sand produced by the crushing process on the mine Washing Floors was washed down the river and deposited by the tides onto the beach. The deep ruts from the wheels of horse drawn carts can be seen leading across the sand in this view dating from the mid 1890s. A solitary changing hut and some rowing boats stand deserted on the beach. The cottage in the foreground later became the End Café. (Photo: Collection, Brian McMullen)

Fishing from boats available for hire on the beach was a popular pastime for visitors, although rowing these fairly substantial examples through the sometimes strong tides must have been rather strenuous! Stone and shingle are now much more evident in this photograph taken some fifteen years later than the previous picture. For many years, Captain Rowe's family held a licence to remove sand and shingle from the beach on payment of a royalty to the Crown. Following closure of the mine, the continued removal of sand caused controversy and the practice eventually ceased. (Photo: Collection, Brian McMullen)

13

James Henry stands outside his somewhat grandiosely named Laxey Restaurant which stood on the sea front in the vicinity of the present day promenade shelter and grassed area. His daughter Nellie married James McCormick, the family running the sea front cafe of the same name until the 1980s. (Photo: Collection, Edith Quaggin)

The caption on the picture helpfully records that the Daisy was Laxey's first motor boat but unfortunately no other information is known. (Photo: Collection, Brian McMullen)

As the Great Laxey Mine edged towards final closure, fewer miners were required and unemployment, especially in the winter months, became a serious problem in the village. A number of winter work schemes were instigated which included the construction of the first part of a proper promenade and sea wall along the sea front in 1929. For the first time neighbouring properties were given some protection from the sea but nevertheless during inshore gales, waves and shingle still wash onto the promenade.
(Photo: Collection, Brian McMullen)

As originally built, the promenade did not reach as far as the End Café which, as this view clearly shows, literally stood on the very edge of the beach. The café closed in the late 1980s and was converted to a private dwelling which is now uninhabitable, somewhat ironically following a landslide which fell from the cliffs to the rear and not by storm damage as would seem more likely. (Photo: Collection, Sue Hutchin)

For centuries an inn or public house has stood next to the old packhorse road where it crossed the river, the present Shore Hotel dating to the early 1800s. Just visible on the lower right of the picture is the horse tramway line which carried ore from the Washing Floors to the harbour until it was removed in 1924. (Photo: Collection, Les Clark)

In 1904 Laxey builder John McKibbin built 'Craigmore' on the site of an old inn known as the Cumberland Arms, at the junction of Tent Road and Old Laxey Hill and directly opposite the Shore Hotel. Used as a tearoom for many years, it later became a printer's workshop. History was to recently turn full circle when a cafe and tea room re-opened but this sadly closed in June 2013.
(Photo: Collection, Ann Haddock)

The Laxey Valley is over three miles long, leading from the beach to the lower slopes of Snaefell, with the Glen Roy valley branching off to the west in the upper village. Dating to the early 1870s, this view is taken from the southern headland of the valley known as South Cape, with Snaefell just visible in the distance. In the foreground are ridges of potatoes which were planted in many small areas of land in the village and which are nowadays, in almost all cases, totally overgrown. (Photo: Authors Collection)

A new main road between Douglas and Ramsey, replacing the old packhorse road, was built in stages during the 1850s and 1860s. The new road around the Laxey Valley from South Cape to Minorca was completed in 1854 and is still known as the New Road to this day! In this view an early example of a motor car, said to belong to the village doctor, is parked on the New Road at South Cape in about 1910. Stopping in the same position today on this blind corner would be fraught with danger, to say the least! Sadly this view of Laxey Valley and the hills beyond is now completely obscured by trees.
(Photo: Collection, Brian McMullen)

Dating to about 1860 this is one of the oldest known photographs of Laxey. From ancient times roads which were little more than rough tracks have led down the hills from Baldhoon, Agneash and, in the foreground, Rencell to meet in the valley bottom and continue onto the beach as the Glen Road. The thatched cottages were demolished when the tramway line was constructed in 1894, the flat ground on the right of the picture now being the site of the Manx Electric Railway's rolling stock storage shed. The newly built Christ Church is prominent on the left of the photograph; it too is now completely obscured by trees.
(Photo: Authors Collection)

19

Construction of the New Road prompted a mini building boom and new shops, pubs and houses were soon built along the sides of the road. Laxey now in effect became two villages; 'Old Laxey' at the beach and 'New Laxey' further up the valley near the mine. One of the first buildings on the approach to 'New Laxey' is the Queens Hotel which was built shortly after the road was completed. The ornate pillars and porch surrounding the front entrance have now unfortunately disappeared. (Photo: Collection, Brian McMullen)

A small boy plays on the roadway outside the shops on the New Road in the early 1900s. A pile of horse manure is the only evidence of the sparse road traffic! Almost any household article, from bread to furniture, could be purchased in the village shops. There was little need for residents to travel outside the village and most didn't. As in almost any rural area, the advent of motorcars and supermarkets would eventually lead to the closure of most of the shops. (Photo: Collection, Brian McMullen)

The 'Big Snow' of February, 1895 was one of the most intense and prolonged snow storms that the Island has ever witnessed. For several weeks, drifts of over twenty feet deep blocked the roads and railways, devastated wildlife and livestock and isolated rural communities. Even the Laxey Wheel came to a halt as the waterwheel became icebound in the freezing temperatures. The photograph shows the New Road once the thaw had begun and village life was beginning to return to normal. (Photo: Collection, Brian McMullen)

Flags and bunting decorate the shops on New Road in celebration of VE Day in May 1945. To the left, Thomas Kinrade stands in the doorway of his bakery. The large Hovis sign on the shop front which projected over the pavement was removed a few years later when Isle of Man Road Services began to operate double deck buses. (Photo: Collection, Edwin Kinrade)

Annie and Eddie Quayle sit on the frontage of their shop on New Road, one of a row of four which were destroyed by fire on 1st April 1937. Annie then moved to a small shop on the other side of new road, trading as M A Kennaugh (her mother's maiden name) until she passed away in 2001 at the age of 96, having traded continuously for nearly 80 years. Judging from the shop window display, Laxey residents evidently enjoyed Bird's Custard and Bourneville Cocoa. Accountant Nicola Bowker's offices now occupy the site of the old row of shops. (Photo: Collection, John Kinrade)

Also constructed shortly after the opening of the New Road, the Commercial Hotel was the most important of the five pubs in the upper village. A large stable block was provided to the rear and the Commercial quickly became the changing point for horses used on the Douglas and Ramsey stage coaches. In 1976 it was renamed 'Ye Olde Coach and Horses' and following a number of years of closure was converted into the Village Health Centre in 2002. In the photograph, a horse drawn jaunting car stands outside the main entrance but the petrol engine has begun to make its presence felt, part of the sign on the roof proclaiming 'motor garage'. (Photo: Collection, Brian McMullen)

One of the most urgent requirements faced by Laxey Village Commissioners following the Local Authority's creation in 1895 was the provision of a mains water supply. Although the village is surrounded by numerous rivers and streams, almost all were subject to existing rights held by the Mining Company and others to use the water for industrial purposes. After extremely lengthy and acrimonious debate, it was decided to use water from the streams at Gretch Vane near Minorca and Strooan ny Quill near Fairy Cottage; within several years the water supply proved inadequate during the summer months. Somewhat incredibly, a number of residents argued against a water supply due to the additional cost to the village rate! Workmen and locals pose for the camera in 1910 during the laying of the water main beneath the New Road. (Photo: Authors Collection)

23

In the early 1960s an Isle of Man Road Services bus and a solitary pedestrian leisurely make their way across the bridge spanning the Glen Roy Valley. Originally known as Moore's Bridge, the viaduct was the biggest engineering obstacle encountered during the construction of the New Road. Prominent to the right is the Working Men's Institute, built in 1877 to 'further the educational and leisure pursuits' of the miners and other workmen. After several decades of dereliction, the building was restored by volunteers and re-opened in May 2011. (Photo: Authors Collection)

Isle of Man Highway Board workmen attend to the road surface on the bridge prior to the construction of a pavement on the downstream side, as seen in the previous photograph. Unfortunately the roadway was then too narrow for the ever increasing volume of traffic and this was remedied by removing the stone walls and constructing new cantilevered pavements on either side. Pedestrians now unknowingly cross the bridge with little more than fresh air beneath their feet! While the work was being carried out, agreement was reached with the MER for pedestrians to walk across the tram bridge, an arrangement which today would undoubtedly raise Health and Safety issues, as would the complete absence of safety equipment being worn by the Highway Board workmen. (Photo: Authors Collection)

Just upstream from the road bridge is the Laxey Glen Mill, constructed in 1860 by Mine Captain Richard Rowe. The mill was designed by Mine Engineer Robert Casement who some six years earlier had built the Laxey Wheel. Although there were a number of traditional corn mills in the village, Rowe identified a potential business opportunity as the population of the village rapidly increased. However, the mill was not as successful as he had anticipated and in November 1879 it was sold to his miller Thomas Corlett. Its subsequent history was quite eventful, being destroyed by fire on three occasions with several periods of temporary closure. In 1973 the Corlett family sold the mill to the Manx Government and it is still in active operation, providing high quality flour for the Island's bakeries and domestic customers. In this pre First World War photograph, two horse drawn carts loaded with sacks of grain stand outside the mill. The chimney to the rear was demolished in January 1924; attempts to drag it to the ground by traction engines failed and the job was completed by dynamite. The Laxey Glen Gardens Pavilion is visible on the right. (Photo: Collection, John Kneale)

A bowling green was laid out in the glen to the rear of the mill in the early 1870s and this provided the impetus for the laying out of the Victoria Park. It was acquired by Laxey businessman Robert Williamson in 1875 and shortly afterwards was renamed the Laxey Glen Gardens. Williamson quickly developed the glen into one of the Islands most popular tourist attractions. Visitors could dine in the pavilion restaurant or sit on its veranda and enjoy afternoon strawberries and cream. There were three bandstands, a wooden dancing floor and a boating lake next to the river. The more energetic visitor could enjoy a game of tennis or for those wishing for a more leisurely pursuit, a bowling green and croquet lawn were laid out. The drawing appeared in an 1881 trade directory and includes, to the lower right, the Williamson family home which was later incorporated into the Glen Hotel. (Photo: Authors Collection)

Entry to the Glen Gardens was by an impressive gateway and turnstile located next to the hotel and which was known by locals as the 'gardens street'. Admission was 6d, a fee which the local youth regularly attempted to avoid by walking down through the adjacent Axnfell plantation. The Laxey Glen Hotel, which Williamson built in 1888, is just visible to the right. It survives today as a residential home for the elderly. Sadly the entrance gates and pillars have long since disappeared. (Photo: Collection, Mike Kelly)

A small wooden 'eating room' was built in 1876. Of largely wooden construction, it was extended on a number of occasions to provide additional dining accommodation and to house an indoor bowling alley. (Photo: Authors Collection)

As the number of visitors rapidly increased, an upper floor with an outside veranda was added in 1897 which was particularly popular with those enjoying afternoon teas. In front of the pavilion, a circular flower bed was laid out to the same size as the Laxey Wheel, complete with red flowers to resemble the colour of the wheel's woodwork. The actual waterwheel can just be seen in the top right of the photograph. A view such as this is impossible today due to the tree growth. (Photo: Collection, Brian McMullen)

The pavilion was completely destroyed by fire in August 1913 and a more substantial replacement was quickly constructed on the same site. In more recent times, in 1982, the building was badly damaged in an arson attack. Although rebuilt and refurbished, the pavilion, at the time of writing, remains empty, a sad reflection of the decline of the glen and tourism in general. (Photo: Collection, Brian McMullen)

Inside the rebuilt pavilion, the dining room could accommodate over 160 people in one sitting. Full roast dinners were available for 2s 6d. (Photo: Collection, Brian McMullen)

For a number of years before the First World War, the Laxey Glen Gardens were tenanted and operated by the Manx Electric Railway which constructed this band stand, viewing area and a cafe in the lower gardens next to the river. Military bands were engaged each season to play daily concerts. The area is now the children's playground. This view is from an official postcard issued by the MER. (Photo: Collection, Brian McMullen)

Next to the pavilion was a sprung dancing floor built from maple wood grown in the glen. A resident band played from an ornate bandstand overlooking the dance floor although by the time of this view, in the immediate pre Second World War period, the bandstand had disappeared. The picture does, however, nicely illustrate the wooden floor boards. Dancing would continue late into the evening, illuminated by acetylene gas lights. Although the lamps standards still survive, the dance floor has long since disappeared. (Photo: Collection, Mike Kelly)

Robert Williamson and his wife Agnes pose for the photographer slightly further up the glen from the band stand area. To their rear, the waterfall was formed by allowing water from the overflow of the Laxey Glen Mill lade to cascade over the rock of the valley side. (Photo: Authors Collection)

A boating lake with another ornate bandstand was constructed in 1894 next to the river immediately to the rear of Laxey Glen Mill. In 1906 it was covered over with wooden boards to form a dancing floor and roller skating rink but very quickly reverted to its previous use. In the early 1990s the bandstand was demolished and the lake was drained and planted with shrubs, the area now being a very sad reminder of its former glory. (Photo: Collection, Brian McMullen)

During the early 1950s, one of the lounges of the Bridge Inn (see opposite) was converted into The Tudor Cocktail Bar, complete with typical decor of the era. (Photo: Authors Collection)

Younger visitors were not overlooked and a playground with hobby horses, swings, roundabouts and slides was provided; several photographs suggest that older visitors also enjoyed the playground attractions! (Photo: Collection, Mike Kelly)

Montague House, now the Laxey Chemist, stands next to the Working Men's Institute and opposite the 'gardens street'. It was built in 1869 and from 1870 until 1880 served as the premises of the Laxey Industrial Co-operative Society which had been formed by a number of the miners. The photograph shows Montague House prior to the realignment of the front of the building with the Working Men's Institute which allowed the road and pavement to be widened. (Photo: Collection, John Corlett)

On the opposite side of the road is the Bridge Inn which was built in 1857. Despite the strenuous efforts of Temperance advocates, some of the Laxey Miners enjoyed an unrivalled reputation as copious drinkers! In about 1902, the Bridge Inn was rebuilt with a frontage formed of red brick which, from the late 1950s, has been painted white. Laxey now has four public houses; twenty years ago there was double that number. (Photo: Collection, Brian McMullen)

The old road leading down from Baldhoon to the Glen was intersected by the New Road and the resultant crossroads is now one of the busiest junctions in the village, although in this immediate post war view traffic is sparse. Looking in the direction of Douglas, the Post Office is prominent. Just visible on the extreme left is the Laxey Industrial Co-operative Society store which was built in 1880 and became the Whitehouse Cafe in 1963. History has come full circle, the building now containing the Laxey branch of the Manx Co-op. (Photo: Collection, Richard Davis)

A number of Laxey's grocers used a horse drawn delivery cart to deliver larger food orders or bulkier items which could not be carried by the purchaser. The Laxey Industrial Co-operative Society's cart was photographed during a typical delivery although unfortunately the location is not known. (Photo: Authors Collection)

The Douglas and Laxey Coast Electric Tramway, later to become the Manx Electric Railway, was opened as far as Groudle on 7th September 1893 and then to Laxey on 28th July 1894. Laxey's original station was at Lower Rencell Hill opposite the present tram shed. The rear of the wooden station building projected over the steep bank and was supported by wooden posts. Car 2 carries a pair of 'bow collectors' to collect current from the overhead wire; these were replaced with trolley poles in 1898. (Photo: Authors Collection)

During the winter of 1895-1896 the tramway was extended to a new station at the rear of the former Isle of Man Bank building. Passengers travelling onto Snaefell summit had to walk through the village to a separate station for the mountain line new station. The Laxey Woollen Mills are prominent in the lower part of the picture and the Laxey Glen Mill in the centre with the Glen Gardens Pavilion to its rear. (Photo: Authors Collection)

The new station was opened to coincide with the completion of the extension of the coastal tramway to Ramsey. The Snaefell Mountain Railway station building at Mines Road was dismantled and rebuilt in the new station and is still in use today. A large wooden 'refreshment and dining' pavilion built at the same time was destroyed by fire in September 1917 and not replaced. An architectural feature of the station was the rustic woodwork which decorated the exteriors of the buildings; the matching wooden seats could be rather uncomfortable dependant on the seating position adopted! (Photo: Authors Collection)

Manx tourism reached a peak of popularity in the years between the two World Wars and the electric tramway carried thousands of passengers on a daily basis during the summer months. Scenes such as this, with long queues of passengers waiting for the Snaefell Mountain Railway, were a daily occurrence. On the busiest days, every item of rolling stock was pressed into service to meet the demand. (Photo: Authors Collection)

The 1904 re-equipment of Laxey power station included the installation of these two 400HP Bellis-Morcom triple expansion steam engines driving two alternators which produced three phase alternating current at 7000 volts. Rotary convertors converted the electricity to direct current as used by the trams. The equipment was all sold as scrap in 1935. Since that time the building has had a wide variety of uses including a carpet making factory and a film studio. It is now used as a builder's warehouse. (Photo: Authors Collection)

At the time of the electric tramway's construction, electrical technology was very much in its infancy and there was no public electricity supply on the Island. The tramway company therefore had to generate its own electricity. An old paper mill in Laxey Glen was acquired and converted into a power station. Electrical technology evolved at a rapid pace and by 1904, when the power station was rebuilt, the generating equipment had become completely obsolete. A 135 feet high chimney, erected in 1921, was the source of constant annoyance to Glen Road residents who complained almost continually about the smoke. In 1935 the MER ceased its own power generation and instead sourced electricity from the recently formed IOM Electricity Board. (Photo: Authors Collection)

Construction of an electric tramway from Laxey to the summit of Snaefell began in January 1895. Progress was rapid and the line opened on 21st August of the same year! It was the first mountain railway in the British Isles. At Laxey, passengers had to climb a long flight of steps from Mines Road to the terminus which was situated next to the tram shed. In 1897 the line was extended down the hillside to Mines Road and in 1898 it was extended again into the present station. In this view taken shortly after opening in August 1895, tramway staff stand with one of the trams near to the tram shed. (Photo: Collection, Ray Stanfied)

During the winter months the tramway operated a much reduced service for local residents. To reduce operating costs, a water powered turbine was installed in 1899 to generate the electricity. A weir was constructed across the Laxey River near the main power station to collect water for the turbine which housed in a new building to the rear of the Shore Hotel. Water was piped to the turbine from a header tank next to the power station. Other than the cost of routine maintenance, electricity could be generated virtually free of charge by the turbine. (Photo: Authors Collection)

On 14th September 1905, motor car racing was taking place on the Mountain Road. As the road was closed the Snaefell Mountain Railway had to operate a shuttle service between Laxey and the Bungalow. On one of the descents to Laxey, the leading tram of a convoy of three stopped at Lhergy Veg. The third tram failed to stop in time and smashed into the rear of the second which in turn was pushed into the first. The resultant damage was substantial as shown in the picture of the tram which caused the incident, its front end being all but destroyed with the underframe and leading bogie being badly bent. Curiously, there is no debris visible, suggesting that the onlookers are viewing the damaged tram at a least a few days after the accident occurred. (Photo: Authors Collection)

At the Ramsey end of Laxey station, the separate lines to Ramsey and Snaefell run parallel out of the station and across New Road. The single section of the Snaefell line, on the left, and the level crossing was controlled by a flagman who was provided with a small wooden hut for shelter. On this occasion as Snaefell tram 6 enters the single line section there is not a single road user or pedestrian to be seen. (Photo: Collection, Brian McMullen)

This small wooden shop was situated at the Ramsey end of the station, next to the level crossing. It was built as a small photography studio by Laxey based photographer Spence Lees but when this picture was taken prior to the Second World War it was being used as a gift shop selling sweets, ice cream and fresh fruit etc. The building was removed in the late 1950s for use on a farm near Glen Roy. (Photo: Authors Collection)

39

Shepherds Café stood on the corner of Captains Hill and New Road. It is possible that the building was originally a public house called the Volunteer Arms which is known to have been located in this area; it certainly shares common architectural features with both the Queens Hotel and the Commercial Hotel. At other times the building was used as a bank and later as an ironmongers shop before being converted to a cafe. It was finally, until July 2014, occupied by Blacks Fireplaces and is now called the 'Spanish Embassy'. (Photo: Collection, Mike Kelly)

For a time during the 1950s the cafe was known as the Cornucopia Café before being renamed as the Corner Cafe. In this picture a procession of children from Christ Church Sunday School makes it way past the cafe with Laxey Brass Band bringing up the rear. Today, a road closure order would be required for a similar procession to be carried out in safety! The wooden building to the right of the café is now the 'Phoenix Takeaway'.
(Photo: Authors Collection)

Immediately on passing Captains Hill, the New Road crosses the Laxey Valley on an embankment originally known as 'Andersons Bridge' below which was the Great Laxey Mine's Washing Floors. During the 1870s, nearly 400 men and a few women and children worked on the Washing Floors operating the machinery which separated the lead and zinc ores from the waste stone. Built in 1848, the Washing Floors were extended in 1861 and this rare photograph shows the work being carried out. On the upper right is the Mine Captain's house which is now the Mines Tavern; Captain was a Cornish mining term denoting the mine manager. Christ Church is also visible, the absence of trees again being noteworthy. (Photo: Authors Collection)

Following the liquidation of the Mining Company in 1920, the mine remained closed for two years until it was purchased and reopened by Robert Williamson. Although Williamson died in 1927 his family continued to operate the mine, albeit on a much reduced scale, until final closure took place in April 1930. Several months after Williamson took over the mine, the main crushing mill on the Washing Floors was destroyed by fire. The 42 feet diameter waterwheel visible in the photograph was scrapped following closure but in 2006 the wheel pit was re-used for the restoration of the former Snaefell Mine waterwheel. (Photo: Authors Collection)

Ore was originally brought out of the mine in waggons hauled by ponies. In 1877 the ponies were replaced by two tiny 19 inch gauge steam locomotives named Ant and Bee built by Stephen Lewin of Poole. The locomotives ran one mile into the mine along the main level known as the Adit. In this pre First World War view one of the locomotives with a train of empty wagons is pictured in front of the huge heap of 'deads'. Sadly both locomotives were scrapped in 1935 but replicas were commissioned in 2004 by the Laxey and Lonan Heritage Trust which restored the surface section of the tramway. Glen Mooar housing estate was built on the site of the deads heap in the early 1970s. (Photo: Authors Collection)

Looking in the opposite direction to the previous photograph, by 1900 the Washing Floors was dominated by the huge pile of waste stone known as the 'deads'. Wagons filled with waste were raised to the top of the deads for tipping by a lift inside the stone tower known as the Hayman. All the machinery on the Washing Floors was powered by a number of waterwheels although a large steam engine was installed as a standby for use in the summer months when the water supply was insufficient. One of the waterwheels is visible in this picture. The large brick chimney was connected to the boilers of the steam engine. (Photo: Authors Collection)

Despite the Great Laxey Mine being one of the richest and most celebrated metal mines in Britain, photographs, other than of the Laxey Wheel, are extremely rare. This photo of a boodle on the Washing Floors is thus historically invaluable. Boodles were used to separate finely crushed ore which was firstly tipped onto a central cone. Water from revolving brushes, powered by the waterwheel, caused the ores to separate into concentric rings on the cone due to their differing densities. Here a workman is about to unload ore which has undergone the separation process into a wheel barrow. (Photo: Authors Collection)

43

It is difficult today to imagine the appalling working conditions which the miners endured on a daily basis. Working shifts were eight hours long, six days each week with the only paid holidays being Good Friday and Christmas Day; the average weekly wage was only 21s. Underground the conditions were humid, wet and muddy. The lowest workings were over 2200 feet deep and were accessed by descending wooden ladders. Lighting underground was entirely by candle and the only protective clothing worn were felt hats stiffened by smearing clay on the outside. In the photograph, taken at the Mines Yard, some of the miners are carrying extra candles, tied together by their long wicks. To their rear, mounted on a pole, is the bell which was rung to signal the start of each shift. (Photo: Authors Collection)

In this pre First World War view from the top of the Deads, part of Dumbells Row which was built in the late 1860s, can be seen on the left of the picture, with Mines Road leading on towards the Laxey Wheel. In the centre is the Mines Yard where the mine workshops were situated. The Laxey River is almost dried out, the water having been diverted to operate the waterwheels and machinery on the Washing Floors. (Photo: Authors Collection)

In 1907 the miners staged a brief strike in protest over proposals to change their terms and conditions. The dispute was quickly resolved and the miners soon returned to work. Laxey photographer Spence Lees, whose studio was directly opposite the Mines Yard, was able to photograph a group of strikers. To their rear is the 'Changing House' where the miners could wash and change into clean clothes prior to going home. (Photo: Authors Collection)

Visitors making their way to the Laxey Wheel walked along Dumbells Row and enterprising residents quickly opened small cafes in their front rooms. At one time all 20 houses were said to be serving food or refreshments, the most popular meal being 'Ham and Egg'; the row is still known as 'Ham and Egg Terrace' to this day. Today, only one cafe remains, the former Brown's Cafe now known simply as 'Laxey's'. In this 1950s photograph, members of a cycling club meet at the café for refreshments. (Photo: Collection, Norman McKibbin)

Despite having only rudimentary facilities and a small oil fired stove in the tiny kitchen to the rear, Brown's Cafe provided hundreds of quality meals, from sandwiches to full roast dinners, on a daily basis. In this picture from 1930, fish is being prepared on a wooden table in the open yard to the rear of the café.
(Photo: Collection, Norman McKibbin)

Brown's Café was also a very popular venue for many other functions, a trade which was particularly important during the winter months. In this view, the dining area has been prepared for a wedding reception, the wedding cake occupying pride of place on the top table. (Photo: Collection, Norman McKibbin)

Numerous other fairground type attractions, such as coconut shies, hoop la and archery, also appeared along Mines Road to tempt the visitor to part with their holiday money! At Spence Lees photography studio visitors could be photographed against backcloths of Peel Castle or Laxey Wheel, or sitting in a mock up of an early motor car; all can be seen in this pre First World War photograph of the studio. By the time they had returned from the Laxey Wheel, photographs would be ready for collection!
(Photo: Authors Collection)

Mines Road was part of the ancient roadway which led down from Agneash, a small hamlet on the hills above Laxey. The Laxey River was crossed by a ford in front of the Ballacowle Mill, just upstream from the river's confluence with the Mooar stream. Prior to the construction of a bridge in 1890, the river was frequently impassable in the winter months; farmers complained that they had to take livestock through a long detour above Minorca to reach Agneash. Laxey Wheel and a number of thatched cottages can be seen higher up the hill. (Photo: Collection, Mike Kelly)

In 1890 a small tramway, known as the 'Browside', was constructed from near the Ballacowle Mill leading up to the Laxey Wheel. It was worked entirely by water power with two trams connected by a wire rope running around a brake drum at the top end. Each tram carried a water tank which was filled at the top of the line until it was heavier than the tram at the bottom. It then descended pulling the other tram upwards. The tank was then emptied and the process repeated. The line closed in 1907 and was dismantled shortly afterwards. (Photo: Authors Collection)

Ballacowle Mill, built in the late eighteenth century, was a typically traditional mill with a wooden waterwheel operating several pairs of grinding stones. The photograph, showing a farmer and his horse and cart outside the mill, was taken in 1911. Despite competition from the much larger Laxey Glen Mill, the Ballacowle Mill did not finally close until the Second World War after which it was converted to form part of an engineering works for Manx Engineers Ltd. Following the relocation of Manx Engineers in April 2009, the complex was converted to a tea room, restaurant and exhibition centre, complete with a replica working waterwheel. It is now known as the Ballacregga Tearooms and Salmon Centre. (Photo: Collection, Mike Kelly)

This photograph, dating to 1907, shows the foot of Wheel Hill looking back towards Laxey with the rear of the Ballacowle Mill to the right and the miller's house directly opposite. The reservoir to the rear of the mill was built in 1875 by the Mining Company to store water for the Washing Floors. Water for the mill was taken from the nearby Glen Mooar River and part of the wooden supply lade can be seen passing over the reservoir. Further down the valley the 'deads' tower over the nearby houses. (Photo: Collection, Mike Kelly)

One of the many small cafes on Mines Road and Wheel Hill was run by the Condra family at Hollybank, one of the nearest houses to the Laxey Wheel. Sweets, ice creams and drinks could be purchased from this small roadside kiosk while meals were served in one of the ground floor rooms. As recently as the mid 1970s there were still eight such cafes or tea rooms between the tram station and Laxey Wheel. (Photo: Collection, Irene Simpson)

49

Built in 1897, the Wheel Cafe was of wooden construction with an extremely ornate finish. Sadly, similar care was not taken in choosing its location; it was extremely close to the wheel, almost completely blocking the view from the Wheel Hill side and the Snaefell Mountain Railway. The café was destroyed by an intense fire in November, 1985 which consumed the wooden structure within minutes. The bicycle was probably pushed up the very steep hill; descent, however, would have been much more rapid! (Photo: Authors Collection)

It is not difficult to appreciate why the Laxey Wheel is one of Island's most popular visitor attractions. This superb example of Victorian engineering has a diameter of 72 feet 6 inches, a circumference of 227 feet and a width of six feet and is the largest working waterwheel in the world. Designed by the Mining Company engineer Robert Casement, a native of Laxey, it took nearly five years to build and was used to pump flood water from the lowest depths of the mine. Christened Lady Isabella in honour of the wife of the Island's then Governor, Sir Charles Hope, the waterwheel was formally set in motion at an Opening Ceremony held on 27th September, 1854. This is one of the oldest known photographs of the Lady Isabella, which predates work that took place in 1877 to strengthen the wooden spokes by the addition of a cast iron ring and tie rods. (Photo: Collection, Mike Scarffe)

Photographed from the opposite side, the architectural features incorporated to embellish the waterwheel are clearly evident. The decorative arches, both open and closed, on two levels; the Three Legs of Man emblem; the tower with the spiral staircase and the whitewashed stonework all contribute to give the waterwheel an appearance unrivalled elsewhere. From an engineering perspective a simple stone structure would have sufficed but without doubt the Lady Isabella would not have been such a popular tourist attraction and very likely would not have survived the closure of the mine. The thatched cottage in the foreground was the home of the author's great-great-grandfather and his family. (Photo: Collection, Mike Scarffe)

Edwardian tourists explore the Glen Mooar River to the rear of the Lady Isabella. Photographs of the waterwheel from this angle are rare and this excellent example shows to great effect the tower with its external spiral staircase used to access the top viewing platform. Much more importantly, the tower also housed the internal supply pipe which carried water from a cistern on the nearby hillside to the top of the waterwheel. It is almost as if Robert Casement wanted visitors to wonder how the water was supplied to the top of the wheel, as indeed they still do to this day. (Photo: Authors Collection)

An unusual effect has resulted from the fairly long shutter speed of the camera used to photograph the revolving waterwheel. It does, however, highlight the cast iron 'strengthening ring' added to the spokes in 1877. (Photo: Collection, Mike Scarffe)

For those who are not afraid of heights, the top viewing platform gives excellent views of Laxey Village and the valley leading up to Snaefell. In the foreground is the now demolished Cronk E Chule farmhouse and beyond that the Mines Road and Mines Yard, the latter having a stack of timber stored near the joiners shop. (Photo: Collection, Brian McMullen)

Another of Laxey's ancient roadways led from the harbour, up the northern side of the valley to Slieu Ruy and the other hills beyond Agneash. Grouped around the lower part of the old road, the houses of Minorca were a separate hamlet when this photograph was taken in 1905. Minorca Primitive Methodist Chapel is particularly conspicuous, its size indicating its importance to the small rural community. Another chapel, the Glen Road Wesleyan, can be seen to the lower left of the picture. (Photo: Collection, Brian McMullen)

I.O.M. MINORCA & KING ORRY.   AXNFEL SERIES. 146.

Within a few years of the closure of the Great Laxey Mine in 1930, almost all of the mining machinery had been dismantled by scrap merchants. Fortunately the Lady Isabella remained untouched and in 1937 when demolition again seemed a certainty, the waterwheel was saved by the actions of a young Laxey builder Mr Edwin Kneale. On 27th September, 1954 the Lady Isabella's centenary was celebrated. A procession of schoolchildren and villagers dressed in Victorian costume made its way from the beach to the wheel where a commemorative plaque was unveiled. Mr Kneale stands on the left of the official party with the Island's governor Sir Ambrose Dundas Flux Dundas fourth from the right. A commemorative plaque unveiled by Lady Dundas is still in place on the wheel case. (Photo: Authors Collection)

53

Manx Electric Railway Winter Saloon 19 climbs out of Minorca towards Laxey Old Road crossing, the original Packhorse Road, on its way to Ramsey in the late 1950s. Snaefell Mountain is visible in the distance. Today a scene such as this is impossible as the area is completely obscured by trees, whilst the fields above and below the tramlines have been developed with housing. (Photo: Authors Collection)

Minorca Vale, on the upper part of Minorca Hill, photographed before the construction of the electric tramway and Minorca Bridge took place in 1898. Much of the land is being used for growing potatoes and other vegetables. It is evidently a warm day as linen sheets have been laid out on the bank next to one of the cottages to dry. The Minorca Primitive Methodist Chapel is again a prominent feature of the photograph. (Photo: Authors Collection)

Small cafes or refreshment rooms could be found in many places throughout the village which from today's viewpoint, would seem to be unlikely locations. This small example was situated midway along the Glen Road, presumably for the benefit of those weary visitors who perhaps had not anticipated the fairly lengthy walk between the village and beach. (Photo: Authors Collection)

THE FLOOD AT LAXEY SEPT 18 1930

On the evening of 17th September 1930, the sky over Laxey turned an unusual purple colour before rain began to fall. Light at first, the rain then fell torrentially throughout the night. The following morning villagers awoke to the aftermath of the worst flood in living memory. Although damage had been caused along the length of the rivers, the Glen Road area was the worst affected. Debris from the Deads was washed downstream blocking the MER's weir and forcing the combined water of the Laxey, Glen Roy and Glen Mooar Rivers onto the Glen Road and into adjacent properties.
(Photo: Authors Collection)

Looking in the opposite direction to the previous photograph, the MER's damaged weir, with part of the counterweight mechanism raised, can be clearly seen. Stone from the Deads litters the river bank. In an ensuing court case, the MER was held responsible for the damage and was compelled to pay compensation to effected households and meet the cost of the repairs. In retrospect the verdict was perhaps a little unfair as it seemingly ignored the damage that was caused to the Laxey Wheel and Glen Gardens which were much further up the valley and in which the railway's weir had played no part.
(Photo: Authors Collection)

SOME OF THE VICTIMS OF THE FLOOD AT LAXEY SEPT 1930

Glen Road residents photographed during the clearing up process following the 'great flood' as it became known. Damaged furniture lies on the roadway while one of the ladies on the left of the picture appears to be wearing wet clothing. Judging from the children's expressions, the event was somewhat of an adventure although, no doubt, their parents' thoughts would have been somewhat different. (Photo: Collection, Brian McMullen)

At Laxey Harbour, the scouring effect of the flooded river undermined the foundations of the pier, causing the collapse of a large section of the structure and forcing the temporary closure of the harbour. (Photo: Collection, Brian McMullen)

THE FLOOD DAMAGE AT LAXEY WHEEL SEPT 18 1930

Further up the valley part of the Rod Duct, the structure which carries the wooden connecting rod from the Laxey Wheel to the Engine Shaft, was completely washed away where it crossed the Glen Mooar river. The wooden rods were left hanging in the air and the supporting wheels disappeared into the river and were never seen again. The damage was repaired using simple concrete pillars which are now of historic interest in their own right, having stood longer than the original arches which they replaced! (Photo: Authors Collection)

Until the construction of the New Road prompted the expansion of the village, small thatched cottages with whitewashed stone walls were the typical rural dwelling. Inside there were two rooms and an attic sleeping area with very limited head room beneath the thatch. An end window of the attic area is visible in this picture of Ballacowle Cottage located on the hairpin corner of the Agneash Road. Today the cottage has been considerably enlarged. (Photo: Authors Collection)

59

Ivydene on Wheel Hill is a typical example of the larger two storey cottage which evolved from the earlier thatched cottages and can be seen throughout Laxey and elsewhere on the Island. Ivydene itself had been a thatched cottage which was enlarged and rebuilt in the late 1870s; it can be seen in its original form on the photograph on page 47. (Photo: Authors Collection)

The occupier of this cottage on the Glen Road stands proudly outside her home for the photographer. Of particular note is the wooden vestibule which gave the front door some protection from the elements; some old Manx cottages had a similar structure formed from large slabs of slate. A wooden extension to the left of the cottage would appear to be one of the ubiquitous refreshment rooms. (Photo: Authors Collection)

Alma House, now known as Hillcrest, on the Baldhoon Road was reputedly built as a gift to Robert Casement by the Mining Company following the completion of the Laxey Wheel. However, Casement actually lived in the adjacent Alma Cottage although Alma House did have a mining connection. It is possible that it may have been the original Vicarage for Christ Church before becoming the home of one the senior mine managers. A notable feature is the stone archway in the cellar which supports the ground floor timbers, and which replicate the style of the arches of the rod duct connected to the waterwheel. (Photo: Authors Collection)

The Mine Captain was provided with a large house which still survives as the Mines Tavern next to the tram station. In 1898, part of the house was demolished to allow the tramway extension to Ramsey to run out of the new station. At the same time, Captain Reddicliffe moved to The Sycamores, a newly constructed house on the Ramsey Road. His successor at the mine, Captain John Roberts, lived at Bryn Terion also on the Ramsey Road where he is pictured standing outside with his wife and daughter. The house is now known as Highcliffe. (Photo: Authors Collection)

Sea Level is a fairly substantial three storey house situated, as the name would suggest, near to Laxey beach. It stands on Back Shore Road which until fairly recently was known as 'Pig Street' recalling the area's connection with the old Laxey Fair.
(Photo: Authors Collection)

Glamorgan House at South Cape was built towards the end of the nineteenth century at a cost of £1000 and is reputedly named after Glamorgan in Australia. Unusually only one side of the property features bay windows suggesting that these may have been a later addition. The extent of decoration applied to the exterior is noteworthy. (Photo: Authors Collection)

Constructed high on the valley side at Rencell in 1890, Axnfel was a 19 bedroom hotel which had unrivalled views across the Laxey Valley. Contemporary adverts described the health benefits to hotel guests, one noting that the hotel was only several minutes walk from the beach which, even for the most energetic guests, was an impossible feat! The hotel later became a Youth Hostel and following closure in 1985 is now a private residence. (Photo: Collection, Brian McMullen)

As the Great Laxey Mine declined, many miners emigrated particularly to the South African Mines. Although wages were much higher overseas, many miners contracted lung diseases from the dust and died at an early age. Edward Lawson had emigrated to South Africa and used the money he had earned to build Bay View Terrace in 1907. Sadly in 1911 he too was to die from respiratory problems. The scaffolding being used by the workmen attending to the end gable would undoubtedly fail to meet today's more demanding Heath and Safety standards. (Photo: Collection, Brian McMullen)

Although temperance advocates fought a constant campaign with many of the Laxey Miners, for most religion was a great influence on both their working and social lives. Christ Church has already been mentioned but Methodism also had a strong presence in the village especially in the rural areas, numerous Primitive and Wesleyan chapels being constructed throughout the Parish. Many of the miners were said to attend both church and chapel services on a Sunday. The Glen Road Wesleyan Chapel was constructed in 1850 and during that year nearly 120 children were enrolled in its Sunday School. The chapel closed in 1966 and is now a private residence. (Photo: Authors Collection)

Minorca Primitive Methodist Chapel, built in 1870, was the largest chapel in the village and parish. It too closed in 1966 when the Glen Road Wesleyan and the Minorca Chapels combined to use the Minorca Sunday School building which is now the only active chapel in the village. Following a number of uses, the old Minorca chapel has now also been converted to a private dwelling. (Photo: Collection, John Kinrade)

In addition to the regular church and chapel services, numerous social events, such as musical concerts and the annual Sunday School picnics, were also held which invariably attracted large numbers of attendees many of whom would have walked considerable distances. The photograph, helpfully dated 14th March 1907, shows the Baldhoon Chapel's Annual Bachelors Ball which was held in the barn of the nearby Ballagare Farm. The last service was held at Baldhoon Chapel in 1936. (Photo: Collection, Brian McMullen)

Lonan Wesleyan Chapel at Ballabeg was built in about 1797 on the site where John Wesley had preached in 1781. In 1906 a new Sunday School and hall was constructed and the photograph shows the official ceremony of laying the foundation stone. Both chapel and hall closed in 1980 and the chapel is now a private dwelling. An inscription on the end gable still recalls John Wesley's visit.
(Photo: Authors Collection)

Lonan Parish Church, dedicated to St Adamnan, was built in 1733 to replace the much older and smaller St Adamans Church which dates to about 450AD. The location of the Parish Church, somewhat remote from the expanding village, led to the construction of Christ Church which was granted parish status in its own right in 1917 by the Lord Bishop. (Photo: Collection, Brian McMullen)

The waters of the Glen Roy and Laxey rivers converge slightly
further down the valley from the junction of the old roads, which
have already been described. Laxey River to the right is crossed by
Moughtins Bridge which now has metal railings to increase visibility
for road users. Moughtins Corn Mill stood on the downstream side
of the bridge and in 1881 was converted into the St Georges
Woollen Mills by Egbert Rydings a proponent of the work of John
Ruskin. In 1836 the first school in the parish was provided by the
Church and it is perhaps not a coincidence that it was located near
to the road junction. Before the construction of Christ Church,
services were held in the school which is visible to the left of the
picture. (Photo: Collection, Brian McMullen)

By the mid 1860s, as the village rapidly expanded, the school could
no longer accommodate the increasing number of children. With the
financial assistance of the Mining Company and the National
Society for Education a new school was built on the Ramsey Road.
The old school became the Infants School and in this photograph a
class of at least 52 pupils are present. Most of the children are not
looking to the camera but to their left where presumably their teacher
was standing! (Photo: Authors Collection)

In this pre First World War photograph, one of the National School classes and their teacher pose for the official photographer on the Ramsey Road to the rear of the school. The volume of today's road traffic is such that adopting a similar position would be rather hazardous to say the least. In the present day era of mass digital photography it is difficult to appreciate the importance of school photographs such as this to parents. (Photo: Authors Collection)

Education within Lonan and Laxey was eventually centralised in the present day Laxey Primary School which opened on 10th January, 1929. South Cape and Ballagawne schools were closed and are now private houses; the infant school became a hall for Christ Church and has similarly been recently converted to a private house. The National School was not as fortunate and was demolished soon after closure; only a small part of the rear wall survives adjacent to the main road. (Photo: Authors Collection)

Local authorities were required to provide a fire fighting service within their area but progress, in the rural areas in particular, was exceedingly slow. In Laxey, improvements only came about following a number of serious fires, the Commissioners being compelled to respond to the public outrage expressed in the aftermath of each incident. On 11th February 1905 the Queens Hotel was completely destroyed after an ember fell from an open fire. In the absence of a mains water supply, volunteers carried buckets of water from the Laxey River, some distance away at the foot of Rencell Hill, which were bravely, and completely ineffectively, thrown onto the fire. (Photo: Authors Collection)

Within minutes, the Queen's Hotel was a raging inferno which quickly consumed the entire interior and left only the four stone walls standing. Fortunately the hotel was insured and was quickly rebuilt. (Photo: Authors Collection)

A direct consequence of the fire which destroyed the Laxey Glen Gardens Pavilion in 1913 was the formation of a local fire brigade although this took until May 1914 to achieve. Consisting of 12 volunteers the brigade was ill trained, ill equipped and membership was irregular. Its ineffectiveness was demonstrated in September 1917 when the wooden pavilion in Laxey station was completely destroyed. The photograph shows the Laxey Glen Gardens staff standing amidst the remains of the destroyed pavilion. (Photo: Authors Collection)

In January 1921 a major fire destroyed the Glen Mill. At this time the brigade's equipment consisted of only a fire hose, a few hand pumps and wellingtons and helmets for the firemen. Despite their brave efforts, the mill was very quickly reduced to the four stone walls and a pile of smouldering embers. In the photograph, the Laxey Brigade can are standing on the shed to the left training the solitary hose onto the smouldering building. The assistance of the Douglas Brigade was requested but the building was virtually destroyed by the time they arrived in the village. (Photo: Collection, Brian McMullen)

On the evening of 17th April, 1930 the Manx Electric Railway's tram shed next to Rencell Hill was destroyed in a serious fire which also threatened adjacent properties. Widespread public condemnation of the inadequacies and somewhat haphazard attitude towards the fire fighting provision followed. Finally, a properly trained and equipped fire brigade was formed. The photograph shows the aftermath of a fire in March 1931 which destroyed the shops on New Road belonging to Robert Williamson; the building was repaired and became the offices of Laxey Village Commissioners. No photographs are known to exist of the aftermath of the tram shed fire. (Photo: Authors Collection)

Following the outbreak of the Second World War, Laxey finally took delivery in 1940 of its first motorised fire tender which was supplied by the Local Government Board. Unfortunately it was underpowered and was unsuitable for the steep hills around the village. It was replaced in May 1942 by a new appliance registered FMN 249 and based on an Austin van, together with a tender pump capable of pumping 500 gallons of water per minute. The Laxey Fire Brigade are pictured with the tender and pump in the Laxey Glen Gardens after winning first prize in a wartime competition involving all the Island's brigades. FMN 249 remained in service until 1955. (Photo: Collection, John Kinrade)

On 1st January 1960, the fire authorities outside the Douglas area were amalgamated. In June of the same year, a Dennis F28 tender registered 1817 MN was supplied new to Laxey. It is pictured shortly after delivery parked outside the fire station on Mines Road which was built in 1943 for the wartime Austin. Incorporating an old smithy to the rear, it was little more than a garage and the fire engine could only just fit inside. In 1982 a much needed purpose built fire station was commissioned on the site of the former Mines Yard. The Laxey and Lonan Heritage Trust gift shop and information centre now occupies the old fire station. (Photo: Authors Collection)

Laxey fire brigade pictured with 1817 MN at Laxey football pitch in the mid1960s. (Photo: Authors Collection)

Until 1929, the steam and electric railways enjoyed a virtual monopoly of public transport outside the Douglas area. This was to come to a somewhat abrupt end in 1929 when Cumberland Motor Services set up a Manx subsidiary trading as Manxland to operate bus services throughout the Island. To counter this 'outside' threat a number of local companies almost immediately set up in opposition, the Isle of Man Railway taking a financial interest in Manx Motors Ltd. One of their white liveried 20 seat Thornycroft A2 buses is pictured outside the Laxey Glen Hotel with passengers and staff. (Photo: Authors Collection)

The Isle of Man Railway quickly withdrew from Manx Motors and set up its own company Isle of Man Road Services. With three companies and the railways competing on the major routes the 'bus wars' began. Within months, Isle of Man Road Services was to emerge as the victor and the other companies soon ceased trading. Manx Motors had converted an old stable to the rear of the Commercial Hotel into a garage but this burnt down in December, 1929. In 1933 IOMRS built a new and larger garage on the New Road near to the Deads. An existing house, Snaefell View, became an office and waiting room. It was said that the house was so named as the Island's highest peak could be seen from the waiting room through a crack in the end gable! Note the luggage rack on the roof of the nearest bus, MAN 452, a Leyland Lion dating to 1935. (Photo: Collection, Ray Stanfield)

A Scottish military band parade in full traditional regalia parade outside the bus garage in August 1936; unfortunately the circumstances of the event have long been forgotten. (Photo: Authors Collection)

Following changes to Highway Board legislation in 1947, the use of buses with more than 34 seats outside the Douglas area was permitted for the first time. IOMRS had acquired its first double decker in 1946 but the Laxey garage was too low to accommodate the new vehicles. The roof and doors were then raised in height and the extra section added to the top of the doors is clearly visible. GMN 777 was a 56 seat Leyland Titan PD1 purchased new in 1947. Laxey Bus Station closed in 1969 and was acquired by Princes Motors Ltd as a repair workshop and garage. (Photo: W Barlow)

The walk between the Lady Isabella and the beach is a fairly lengthy one, particularly for visitors with limited time to spend in the village. Recognising this, Reuben Hardy of the Fairy Cottage Filling Station introduced a mini bus service between the wheel and beach in 1962. Mr Hardy is pictured driving one of his mini buses 5413 MN a 12 seat Morris which was new in 1960. The service was taken over by A & R Caine in July 1969 and then by Henry Midghall in June 1973 who continued the service until 1985. By this time it had the distinction of being the only stage carriage bus service operated on the Island other than by the now nationalised bus undertaking. (Photo: Authors Collection)

A familiar sight for many years on the Island's roads was the immaculately presented fleet of Foden lorries of the Laxey Glen Mill which delivered flour and animal feedstuffs to bakers and farmers. LMN 253 was new in July 1949 and is shown loaded with sacks of flour. Fortunately two of the mill's later Fodens, PMN 208 and YMN 741, have been preserved on the Island and restored to as new condition. (Photo: Collection, Mike Kelly)

The steep sides of Laxey Valley were not particularly suitable for farming.
However, many old pictures show land being used for growing crops and
grazing livestock which is today completely overgrown. Prior to the
opening of the Laxey Mine, most of the villagers eked out a poor living by
fishing and also farming small crofts which generally possessed only a few
acres of land. As the mine flourished, the increasing population ensured a
continuing demand for food stuffs and crops, in particular potatoes, were
grown in many places on the valley sides. In this view, dating to about
1896, labourers are harvesting a vegetable crop from the steep land
between the Glen Road and Ramsey Road. This area is now developed
with housing. (Photo: Collection, Brian McMullen)

Again dating to the mid 1890s, this picture shows harvesting to be well underway on fields in the Minorca area. Today, these fields are similarly developed with modern housing or overgrown with vegetation. In the valley, smoke belches from the chimney of the Manx Electric Railway's Glen Road power station. (Photo: Collection, Ian and Sally McMullen)

A number of farmers had daily milk rounds with regular customers throughout the village. Milk was carried in metal churns on the back of a small horse drawn cart and as there were no bottles or cartons, the milk was measured and poured into the purchasers own jugs or jars. Bobby and Willy Clague of Balyolghane Farm at Agneash delivered milk to customers as far from the farm as the beach area. A sledge was kept to ensure that the milk was delivered even if the roads were blocked with snow. The brothers are pictured in March 1937 with the horse and sledge near the Ballacowle Mill on Wheel Hill. (Photo: Collection, Margaret Sadler)

Members of the Clague family of Ballagawne Farm hand pick potatoes being grown in the fields below the main road at Garwick prior to the Second World War. The former Ballagawne School is just visible in the background. (Photo: Collection, Linda Clague)

Farmer Gordon Maggs uses more modern methods to plough fields on the Gretch Voar Farm. On the other side of the valley houses on Mateland Drive, off the Baldhoon Road, are under construction dating the photograph to the early 1950s. Ard Reayrt residential estate now occupies the fields being worked in the photograph. (Photo: Authors Collection)

In 1900 Robert Williamson built two new shops on the New Road which today are more usually recalled as the former branch of the Manx Co-operative. A bakehouse to the rear of the new shops had been built four years earlier in 1896 and was the most modern and well equipped in the village. Three of Williamson's bakers are pictured on New Road outside the bakery which was destined to be the last in operation in the village and closed in 1973. (Photo: Authors Collection)

The final selection of photographs briefly illustrates a small aspect of the social side of Laxey's history. In a scene doubtless carried out on a daily basis throughout the village, a resident of Victoria Terrace on the Glen Road washes a door mat placed on the wall at the rear of her cottage. On the other side of the wall is the Laxey River with the weir for the MER's turbine house just visible. (Photo: Collection, Maureen Thornley)

Staff of the Laxey Glen Hotel are pictured outside the hotel's main entrance on the 'Garden's Street'. Built in 1888 by Robert Williamson, the hotel was finished with ornate exterior decoration, the detail and finish of the balustrades on the steps leading up to the hotel entrance being particularly noteworthy. The hotel is now occupied by a residential home for the elderly. (Photo: Authors Collection)

In May 1907 the recently formed Laxey Rifle Club opened a shooting range alongside the Laxey River to the rear of the Ballacowle Corn Mill and mine reservoir. During the Second World War the range was requisitioned for use by the Laxey Home Guard who are pictured during a typical practice session. There were three ranges of differing lengths and until fairly recently the remains of the targets 'butts', which were made from rows of large tin cans filled with sand, could still be seen amongst the undergrowth. (Photo: Collection, John Corlett)

In 1929, the Liverpool based Erskine Clothing Company began manufacturing clothing in the large warehouse on the harbour side. They had been enticed to Laxey with the promise of a cheap electricity supply by the Laxey Electric Light and Power Company which had a generator in the basement of the building. Employees of the 'Erskine', as the factory was commonly known, are shown sitting at their sewing machines at Christmas 1945. Following closure of the 'Erskine', the building was converted in 1965 to a factory manufacturing smoker's pipes. Although now appropriately occupied by a company involved with the supply and manufacture of specialised mining equipment the building is still known affectionately as the 'Pipe Factory' by locals. (Photo: Collection, Norman McKibbin)

King George VI and Queen Elizabeth greet Laxey school children at Laxey Station during a three day visit to the Island in July 1945.
It was the first Royal Visit that the King and Queen had undertaken outside Great Britain since the Second World War had begun.
(Photo: Collection, Norman McKibbin)

Laxey Stationmaster Percy Harris was one of a number of locals who were featured in an episode of the popular radio programme 'Down your Way' recorded in Laxey in June 1949. Percy, who chose the song 'White Wings', is shown being interviewed by presenter Richard Dimbleby about his work for the Manx Electric Railway. Isle of Man Road Services garage can be seen on the opposite side of the road.
(Photo: Collection, Brian McMullen)

The Working Men's Institute was used for a wide variety of social functions. A representative of the Isle of Man Electricity Board demonstrates his cake making skills at an electrical appliance exhibition in held there in the early 1950s. The Electricity Board maintained a showroom at the Whitehouse Close until the mid 1970s.
(Photo: Authors Collection)

Another Royal Visit to Laxey, on this occasion by HRH Queen Elizabeth, the Queen Mother in July 1963. In the Valley Gardens, the Queen Mother, is introduced to members of the Laxey Village Commissioners by Chairman Hugh Condra. (Photo: Collection, Irene Simpson)

Following the great success of the 'turning ceremony' held in July 1970 to celebrate the restoration of the Lady Isabella, a Victorian themed Laxey Fair has been held annually ever since at the Valley Gardens. In the first of the revived fairs, Laxey School children are pictured in Victorian Costume, including the author, then aged five, in the centre of the front row dressed as a page boy. The embarrassment evident in the picture is still clearly remembered today! (Photo: Authors Collection)

Laxey Brass Band was formed in the mid 1850s. Many of the members were miners and there were a number of disputes when the Mining Company refused to allow band members leave of absence from work to attend events. The band is pictured on the veranda of the Laxey Wheel Café in June 1907. Built in the style of a wooden chalet, the intricate detail of the woodwork is noteworthy. Sadly, Laxey Brass Band was forced to 'disband' in the early 1980s due to a shortage of members. (Photo: Authors Collection)

95

In addition to the Laxey Brass Band, there were also a number of other village bands, particularly associated with a number of the churches and chapels. During the summer months the Salvation Army Band conducted services each Sunday at a number of locations in the village including Dumbells Row and Laxey Wheel, as shown in the picture. (Photo: Collection, Ann Haddock)

Each summer, a military band was engaged by the Laxey Glen Gardens to play a series of concerts throughout the season. The Band of His Majesty's First Lifeguards are pictured by the main bandstand in the lower part of the Gardens during 1907. (Photo: Collection, Brian McMullen)